First Person
A★M★E★R★I★C★A

DISCOVERY
AND
SETTLEMENT

Europe Meets the NewWorld (1490-1700)

Gene Brown

Twenty-First Century Books

A Division of Henry Holt and Company
New York

Twenty-First Century Books
A Division of Henry Holt and Company, Inc.
115 West 18th Street
New York, New York 10011

Henry Holt® and colophon are trademarks of Henry Holt
and Company, Inc.
Publishers since 1866

©1993 by Blackbirch Graphics, Inc.
First Edition
5 4 3 2 1
Published in Canada by Fitzhenry & Whiteside Ltd.
195 Allstate Parkway, Markham, Ontario L3R 4T8

Printed in the United States of America
All first editions are printed on acid-free paper ∞.

Created and produced in association with Blackbirch Graphics, Inc.

Library of Congress Cataloging-in-Publication Data

Brown, Gene.
    Discovery and settlement: Europe meets the New World, 1490–1700 /
Gene Brown.— 1st edition.
      p. cm. — (First person America)
    Includes bibliographical references and index.
    Summary: Provides primary source materials related to the discovery
and settlement of America and daily life in the colonies, including the
experiences of Native Americans, African Americans, and women.
    ISBN 0-8050-2574-X (alk. paper)
    1. United States—History—Colonial period, ca. 1600–1775—Sources—
Juvenile literature. 2. Minorities—United States—History—17th cen-
tury—Sources—Juvenile literature. 3. Minorities—United States—
History— 18th century—Sources—Juvenile literature. 4. America—
Discovery and exploration—Sources—Juvenile literature. [1. America—
Discovery and exploration—Sources. 2. United States—History—Colonial
period, ca. 1600–1775—Sources. 3. Minorities—History—Sources.] I.
Title. II. Series.
E188.B8 1993
973.2—dc20

                                    93-8537
                                        CIP
                                        AC

Contents

INTRODUCTION

The people described in this book may sometimes seem strange, as if they came from another world. But behind the odd language and old customs are men and women who were simply trying to cope with many difficult situations. As you read their words, you'll realize that, in many ways, they were not so different from modern Americans.

In fact, some of what they wrote, said, and did may have a familiar ring to those of us reading their words today. Even early in our recorded history, there is something present that is already "American." The origins of many of our customs and beliefs are rooted in this period.

Also obvious in the records of our past is the start of a particularly American way of dealing with problems. The colonists whose words you will read here were often willing to try new ways of doing things—more so than people in Europe. The colonists were practical and experimental, as well as rugged and determined, which is how most Americans are viewed even today.

In North America during the early years of the seventeenth century, the New World colonists built a society completely on their own—from the ground up. In European society, people knew their place, and the social structure was well organized, from top to bottom. Tradition governed how life was led, and children grew up to do the same thing their parents did before them. Change came very slowly.

On December 26, 1620, Pilgrims from the *Mayflower* landed at Plymouth Rock, Massachusetts. There, they established the first permanent European settlement in New England (*North Wind Picture Archives*).

When the Europeans came to this country, they brought with them ideas and institutions that were not designed for this new land. Faced with problems they had never encountered, the colonists had to confront new dangers without guidance from the past. They had to adapt what they brought with them to fit life in America. Because of their needs, change became constant and accepted.

The mostly unoccupied American land also played a role in creating a new kind of life. Children did not have to live where their parents lived. They could move, and they often did. People who did not like the way others worshiped in their town could migrate and start their own town. So, almost by accident, America developed freedom of religion, something almost unknown in Europe.

Geography even indirectly affected the colonists' great thirst for education. Surrounded by wilderness, far from home, they made doubly sure that their children did not grow up ignorant. Education became a priority, especially in New England. Though it was meant to keep people within the Puritan church, eventually, it would have the opposite effect. Schools that were created to strengthen tradition later helped to break it.

American inventiveness did not always have positive results. The "Indians," North America's original inhabitants, looked and acted unlike anything the Europeans had ever seen. Having no precedent to fall back on, the new Americans invented their own way of dealing with the Native Americans, but the results were often disastrous. The effects of white colonization on Native American lands crippled Indian societies in ways that are still felt to this day.

The relationship between whites and African Americans was also damaging in a way that has been long-lasting. Slavery would not have fit European farming, but by the end of the century, it did fit well with agriculture in the Southern colonies.

Southern planters came up with many reasons why African Americans belonged in bondage. Whites convinced themselves that "owning" African Americans was reasonable and just. These attitudes and practices—like those toward the Native Americans—created struggle and suffering that continues today.

The European settlers in America were human; they made mistakes and had many unfair practices, but they also accomplished admirable things. As did all immigrants after them, they gathered in groups to help each other survive the hardships of a new life and to cope with the unknown as best they could. After a while, most colonists began to go on their own way, settling new frontiers and conquering new challenges. Their bold and independent spirits continued the tradition of their ancestors.

Their story, like that of so many other non–Native Americans, begins on a ship sailing the Atlantic, with one brave and curious man at the helm.

Christopher Columbus
(*Blackbirch Photo Archives*).

CHAPTER 1

EXPLORATION AND THE FIRST COLONY

The Log of Christopher Columbus

Until the last decade of the fifteenth century, Europeans knew little about the world outside Europe. They may have heard about a possible land to the west, and there was some contact with Asia. Africa, however, was mostly unknown territory. Marco Polo (1254–1324), an Italian, had visited the East at the end of the thirteenth century and had written about what he saw. European merchants had gone there to trade, and missionaries had ventured there to convert the "heathens."

The East had spices and precious stones, much in demand in Europe. But the only way to get them was overland, by caravan, and across the Indian Ocean, the Red Sea, the Black Sea, or the Mediterranean. It was a long, dangerous, and expensive trip.

As the 1490s began, the Portuguese were exploring the African coast, navigating with the compass and astrolabe. The tools enabled them to keep track of where they were and in which direction they were going. Exploration of distant places was becoming more possible. Men were beginning to venture into unknown lands and across uncharted seas to see what they might find.

Christopher Columbus (1451–1506), an Italian navigator, persuaded Ferdinand and Isabella, the monarchs of Spain, to pay for a grand and adventurous expedition he had in mind. Columbus hoped to find a new route to the East and its riches if he sailed across the Atlantic Ocean toward the West. The king and

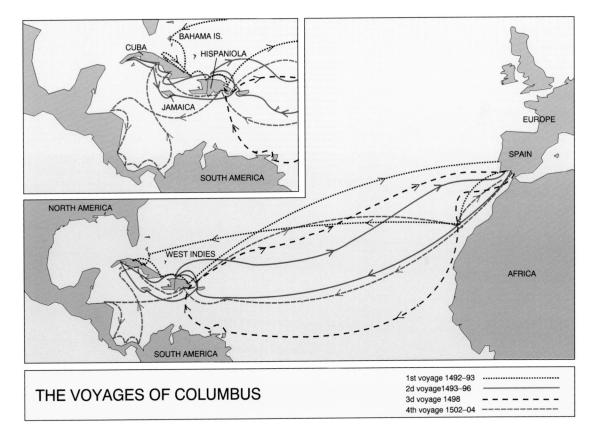

THE VOYAGES OF COLUMBUS

1st voyage 1492–93	·············
2d voyage 1493–96	─────
3d voyage 1498	─ ─ ─ ─
4th voyage 1502–04	── ── ──

queen saw Columbus's journey as a chance to spread Christianity to new lands and to find new sources of wealth that would strengthen their kingdom.

On August 3, 1492, Columbus sailed from Palos, Spain, with 90 men aboard three ships. They stopped at the Canary Islands first and then headed out to sea. Despite popular myth, Columbus and his crew already knew that the world was round: they did not fear that they would fall off the edge. But beyond that, they

Upon his return to Lisbon, Portugal, after his first voyage in 1492–93, Columbus told of great riches and beautiful lands to be found across the Atlantic Ocean (*Library of Congress*).

were sailing on faith. They did not really know where they were going, nor whom or what they might meet. Instead of the facts about geography and ocean currents and detailed maps that are available today, Columbus's men sailed merely with legends, superstition, and their own imaginations.

The expedition was a grueling test of seamanship and faith. Bad weather, sickness, and other constant disappointments quickly sapped the crew of its morale.

What is surprising is not that Columbus's men had second thoughts, as the following selection shows, but that they were willing to finish the voyage at all. They reached the Bahamas on October 12, 1492, ending their long voyage and beginning the recorded history of what we now know as the Americas.

Sunday, 9 September 1492

This day we completely lost sight of land, and many men sighed and wept for fear they would not see it again for a long time. I comforted them with great promises of lands and riches. To sustain their hope and dispel their fears of a long voyage, I decided to reckon fewer leagues than we actually made. I did this that they might not think themselves so great a distance from Spain as they really were. For myself I will keep a confidential accurate reckoning....

I am having serious trouble with the crew, despite the signs of land that we have and those given to us by Almighty God. In fact, the more God shows the men manifest signs that we are near land, the more their impatience and inconstancy increases, and the more indignant they become against me. All day long and all night long those who are awake and able to get together never cease to talk to each other in circles, complaining that they will never be able to return home. They have said that it is insanity and suicidal on their part to risk their lives following the madness of a foreigner. They have said that not only am I willing to risk my life just to become a great Lord, but that I have deceived them to further my ambition. They have also said that because my proposition has been contradicted by so many wise and lettered men who considered it vain and foolish, they may be excused for whatever might be done in the matter. Some feel that they have already arrived where men have never dared to sail and that they are not obliged to go to the end of the world, especially if they are delayed anymore and will not have sufficient provisions to return. I am told by a few trusted men (and these are few in number!) that if I persist in going onward, the best course of action will be to throw me into the sea some night.

From: *The Log of Christopher Columbus,* translated by Robert H. Fuson. (Camden, Maine: International Marine Publishing, 1987). Copyright © 1987 by Robert H. Fuson. Reprinted by permission of International Marine Publishing/TAB Books, a division of McGraw-Hill, Incorporated.

Juan Ponce de León
(*Library of Congress*).

Juan Ponce de León

Spain's official court historian, Antonio de Herrera, wrote that in exploring Florida, Juan Ponce de León (1460–1521) aimed "to gain honor and increase his estate." Like the British who followed them, Spanish explorers were driven by a quest for glory and gold. They, too, wanted to convert the Indians—but to Catholicism, not the Christianity of the Reformation, which was the religion of the British. The Spanish also hoped to find curious and magical places, such as the legendary "fountain of youth."

In the century after Columbus discovered America, Catholic Spain was the strongest power in Europe. Its powerful naval forces ruled the seas, enabling it to colonize the southern part of the New World. By controlling the great waterways, Spain could bring back the gold that kept it strong until late in the sixteenth century.

Spain founded her first colony in Santo Domingo (now the Dominican Republic), on the island of Hispaniola, in 1496. Puerto Rico was next, colonized by Ponce de León in 1509. Then came Cuba. In 1513, at Easter, Ponce de León discovered Florida—almost accidentally, as you will see from the following excerpt. He named it for the Easter holiday (*Pascua Florida,* in Spanish).

Then Vasco Núñez de Balboa (1475–1519) landed on present-day Panama, crossed it, and discovered the Pacific Ocean. In 1519, Hernando Cortés (1485–1547) reached Mexico and within three years had conquered it. Francisco Pizzaro (1475–1541) subdued much of South America in the 1530s, and from 1539 to 1542, Hernando de Soto (1496–1542) explored the present southeastern United States. At about the same time, Francisco Vásquez de Coronado (1510–1554) marched through what is now New Mexico, fighting the Indians along the way.

Despite this activity, early Spanish exploration of what later became the United States did not lead to much influence right away. The very first city founded in what is now the United States was the

The oldest city in what is now the United States is St. Augustine, Florida, originally settled by Spain (*New York Public Library*).

Spanish settlement of St. Augustine, Florida. But a number of Hispanic contributions to American culture came later, when the Spanish colony of Mexico herself colonized the American Southwest and California—areas that were eventually incorporated into the United States. Some of the Spaniards' horses escaped from the colonies to become the ancestors of the wild horses of the western plains—the horses with which the Plains Indians won a brief but glorious epoch in their history.

What follows is Ponce de León's firsthand account of his explorations written in a letter to his king.

Letters to the Emperor
Juan Ponce de León to Charles V.
Documentos inéditos de Indians, Vol. XL. 50–52:
Porto Rico, February 10, 1521

Among my services I discovered, at my own cost and charge, the Island Florida, and others in its district, which are not mentioned as being small and useless; and now I return to that island, if it please God's will, to settle it, being enabled to carry a number of people with which I shall be able to do so, that the name of Christ may be praised there, and Your Majesty served with the fruit that land produces. And I also intend to explore the coast of said island further, and see whether it is an island, or whether it connects with the land where Diego Velázquez is, or any other; and I shall endeavor to learn all I can. I shall set out to pursue my voyage hence in five or six days.

From: Collected Letters of Juan Ponce de León (1521).

Opportunity Across the Sea

I magine that a company has been organized to make a profit from real estate in an area that is not too well known. The company's founders, needing more money, have to persuade more people to invest in the business. The company must also recruit workers to do the dirty work of actually developing the land. To get the money and labor it needs, the company might advertise, showing the area that needs development in the best possible light.

That challenge is something like what confronted the Virginia Company in England in 1609. The company had received the right to develop and exploit part of the New World from the king. The members of the Virginia Company, however, knew that this was a costly and dirty business.

The Company received its charter from Britain's King James I on April 10, 1606. On May 6, 1607, ships carrying about 120 settlers entered Chesapeake Bay. Within a week, they sailed up a river, which they named for their king, and began the first permanent English settlement in America. Over the next several years, in a settlement they called Jamestown, they cleared land, planted crops, built forts, and traded with the Indians. Like the Spaniards before them in Florida and Puerto Rico (meaning "rich port"), they did not intend to start a new society, just to bring back what they believed to be the riches of the New World. But these first English inhabitants of what would become part of the state of Virginia had a much harder time than they'd expected. They fought among themselves and discovered that some of their colleagues were unfit to do the work that had to be done. Crops failed, and the colonists felt constantly threatened by the Indians. Many people were lost to disease, starvation, and the strong desire to return to Europe. To make matters worse, the colonists became disheartened when they finally realized that the great riches and easy life they had hoped for were not going to be a reality.

By 1608, only 38 of the original 120 colonists—led by Captain John Smith (1580–1631)—were left. As a business, the Virginia Company was headed for failure. If the company was to survive, it would have to find new investors and settlers.

A poster advertising the riches of the New World (*Library of Congress*).

17

European explorers were met by Native Americans when they first arrived on the shores of the New World (*Library of Congress*).

In an effort to save itself, the Virginia Company began to spread the word around Europe about the "opportunity" that lay across the sea. The following selection is part of a longer piece that also appeals to the religious feeling and work ethic (belief in the value of work) of potential settlers. Such feelings were stronger then than now, but the message of the "advertisement" is the chance to make one's fortune in a land of unlimited plenty. You may notice that, just like today's advertisements, this ad emphasizes the positive side of the story and tends to ignore the negative.

Nova Britannia, 1609

The country itself is large and great assuredly, though as yet, no exact discovery can be made of all. It is also commendable and hopeful in every way, the air and climate most sweet and wholesome, and very agreeable to our nature. It is inhabited with wild and savage people, that live and lie up and down in troupes like herds of deer in a forest; they have no law but nature, their apparel, skins of beasts, but most go naked; the better sort have houses, but poor ones; they have no arts nor sciences, yet they live under superior command such as it is; they are generally very loving and gentle, and do entertain and relieve our people with great kindness; the land yieldeth naturally for the sustenance of man, abundance of fish, infinite store of deer, and hares, with many fruits and roots.

There are valleys and plains streaming with sweet springs, there are hills and mountains making a sensible proffer of hidden treasure, never yet searched; the land is full of minerals, plenty of woods; the soil is strong and sends out naturally fruitful vines running upon trees, and shrubs: it yields also resin, turpentine, pitch and tar, sassafras, mulberry trees and silkworms, many skins and rich furs, many sweet woods, and costly dyes; plenty of sturgeon, timber for shipping. But of this that I have said, if bare nature be so amiable in its naked kind, what may be hope, when art and nature both shall join and strive together, to give best content to man and beast?

From: *Tracts and Other Papers Relating Principally to the Origin, Settlement, and Progress of the Colonies in North America*, Vol. 1, Peter Force, ed. (Washington, D.C.: Peter Force, 1836–1846).

Ætatis suæ 21. Aº. 1616.

Pocahontas (*National Portrait Gallery*).

Pocahontas and Captain John Smith

One of the most popular legends from precolonial times was about a friendly and loving Indian woman named Pocahontas (1595–1617). Is it true that Pocahontas, daughter of Chief Powhatan, saved the life of the Jamestown colony leader, Captain John Smith, in 1607, when Powhatan wanted to club him to death? Probably not, say the historians, but the tale started with Smith in his 1624 *General History of Virginia*, part of which follows here.

Captain John Smith (*National Portrait Gallery*).

Although countless legends surround her, Pocahontas was real; her actual name was Matoaka. *Pocahontas*, meaning "playful," was her nickname. John Rolfe, an English colonist, met the Indian woman while she was being held hostage during a conflict between the settlers and the Indians. She fascinated him. Rolfe declared himself "in love with one whose education had bin rude, her manners barbarous...." To remedy that situation he married Pocahontas in 1614. She was baptized and took the Christian name Rebecca. The marriage also helped to restore peace with the Indians.

In 1616, Rolfe took his new wife home to England, where she created quite a stir. The English reaction to Pocahontas was a bit complicated. Part of it had to do with her being strange and foreign. Most people in England, even those who were well educated, had little knowledge of Native Americans—many had never met people other than Europeans. Non-Europeans were often imagined to be very "exotic."

In Pocahontas, however, the English saw a pretty Christian, dressed like an English lady, with an English name who was married to an Englishman. Those who met her found her charming and intelligent—even remarkable. Perhaps meeting this strange and attractive woman gave the English ideas about what the benefits of English culture might do for the other "savages" across the Atlantic in America.

Unfortunately, the real story of Pocahontas does not have a happy ending. In 1617, before she could return to Virginia, she died of smallpox. Brokenhearted, John Rolfe did go back to the colony, only to die in an Indian massacre in 1622.

The selection here, from Captain John Smith's letter to the queen of England in 1616, describes the compassion and sweetness of Pocahontas during times of conflict between the white settlers and the Indians. Similar references to Pocahontas in later writings by Smith helped to create the widespread reputation of Virginia's kindest and most "civilized" Native American.

Most Admired Queene

Some ten yeeres agoe being in Virginia, and taken prisoner by the power of Powhatan their chiefe King, I received from this great Salvage exceeding great courtesie, especially from his sonne Nantaquaus, the most manliest, comeliest, boldest spirit, I ever saw in a Salvage, and his sister Pocahontas, the Kings most deare and wel-beloved daughter, being but a childe of twelve or thirteene yeeres of age, whose compassionate pitifull heart, of my desperate estate, gave me much cause to respect her: I being the first Christian this proud King and his grim attendants ever saw: and thus enthralled in their barbarous power, I cannot say I felt the least occasion of want that was in the power of those my mortall foes to prevent, notwithstanding al their threats. After some six weeks fatting amongst those Salvage Courtiers, at the minute of my execution, she hazarded the beating out of her owne braines to save mine; and not onely that, but so prevailed with her father, that I was safely conducted to James towne: where I found about eight and thirtie miserable poore and sicke creatures, to keepe possession of all those large territories of Virginia; such was the weaknesse of this poore Commonwealth, as had the Salvages not fed us, we directly had starved.

And this reliefe, most gracious Queene, was commonly brought us by this Lady Pocahontas. Notwithstanding all these passages, when inconstant Fortune turned our peace to warre, this tender Virgin would still not spare to dare to visit us, and by her our jarres have beene oft appeased, and our wants still supplyed.

From: *Narratives of Early Virginia, 1606–1625*, Lyon Gardiner Tyler, ed. (New York: Charles Scribner's Sons, 1907).

CHAPTER 2

The Puritans

Freedom of Religion

When a house is offered for sale, the newspaper ad might say "needs work," or "handyman's special." This warns buyers to expect some major faults in the building that they will have to fix. By describing it accurately, the seller is likely to find a buyer who will have the skills and the willingness to tackle whatever needs to be done.

As we saw in the Nova Brittania excerpt boasting of the marvels of Virginia, Europeans were not always given an accurate picture of what to expect on the other side of the Atlantic. They did not know what they were "buying" when they boarded a ship to the new land. Because many planned to settle in a colony for the chance to gain riches, the promise of wealth helped them to accept the shortcomings of the new land and put up with a good deal of unexpected hardship.

Public worship was an important part of daily life for the Puritans in the Massachusetts Bay Colony (*North Wind Picture Archives*).

But what if the reason for leaving England was to settle in the new land and stay for good? That was the hope of the Puritans, who had somewhat lofty goals in mind. They wished to build a new society, not for wealth, but for the freedom to practice their religion in peace. They were also inspired by the idea of having a new land to themselves, where their society could be built from the ground up. This way, every aspect of their colony could be guided by the fundamental principles of their religion.

The Puritans knew that America offered vast stretches of undeveloped land, fruit for the picking, and unlimited wildlife that could be hunted for food. But they also knew that clearing the land, dealing with harsh weather, negotiating with the different tribes of often unfriendly Indians, surviving disease and loneliness far from loved ones, and having the patience to put up with years of slow economic progress and disappointment would put them through a long and difficult ordeal.

In 1630, almost 850 Puritans left England to live by the principles of their religion on Massachusetts Bay. In less than a year, 200 had returned to England, and another 200 were dead from various diseases. The colony needed new settlers, but those who came had to have a realistic idea of what they were going to find.

The Puritans did not want to attract the wrong kind of people. If life were described as too easy, those who signed up for the voyage might include the lazy and unskilled. Although these people would raise the overall population of the settlement, they would not be able to help themselves and could not contribute very much to the well-being of the Massachusettes Bay Colony as a whole.

Unlike Virginia, the Massachusetts Bay Colony was settled by families who hoped to build permanent communities. The new land, they hoped, would be their new home for a long time to come. Thomas Dudley (1576–1653) was a founder of the colony. Later he would serve several terms as governor. The following excerpt is from his letter to a friend in England. Because it is meant to give a realistic picture of what life in the colony was like, Dudley writes not with exaggeration, but with honesty.

Thomas Dudley's Letter to a Friend

If any come hither to plant for worldly ends that can live well at home he commits an error of which he will soon repent him. But if for spiritual and that no particular obstacle hinder his removal, he may find here what may well content him:...materials to build, fuel to burn, ground to plant, seas and rivers to fish in, a pure air to breathe in, good water to drink til wine or beer can be made, which together with the cows, hogs and goats brought hither already may suffice for food, for as for fowl and venison, they are dainties here as well as in England. For clothes and bedding they must bring them with them til time and industry produce them here. In a word, we yet enjoy little to be envied but endure much to be pitied in the sickness and mortality of our people. And I do the more willingly use this open and plain dealing lest other men should fall short of their expectations when they come hither as we to our great prejudice did, by means of letters sent us from hence into England, wherein honest men out of a desire to draw over others to them wrote somewhat hyperbolically of many things here.

From: *Chronicles of the First Planters of the Colony of Massachusetts Bay* by Alexander Young (Boston: C. C. Little and J. Brown, 1846).

Massachusetts Bay Body of Liberties

At first glance, the laws by which the Puritans lived in the Massachusetts Bay Colony might seem exceptionally harsh and even ridiculous. Did they really kill people for worshiping the wrong way? Were people actually executed for practicing "witchcraft," and for cursing? Was a woman punished for being "too familiar" with a man? How did they know people had committed such crimes—did everyone watch everyone else all the time?

To understand what the Puritans were doing, we must first remember that when the Puritans decided to leave England, they sought the freedom to practice *their* religion. They wanted to be guided by their own beliefs without interference from others. But that doesn't mean they would tolerate other beliefs within their midst.

The Puritans wanted to establish a "theocracy," which is a state that enforces God's law as well as human law. While they would have civil officials, such as governors, the ministers and church elders would hold the real power.

What was "proper" was not up to individuals to decide. The elders and the ministers decided what was right for all. What guided these people, often known as "the elect"? Most often it was the Bible, and their interpretation of it. This was the ultimate source of authority, not a constitution and a system of laws as we know them. That's why their "Capitall Laws" quoted the Bible.

If God's word was the source and reason for everything, then going against that word threatened all that the Puritans stood for. They dealt with serious crimes with the ultimate penalty of death. Crimes of a lesser nature, such as women being too "familiar" with men, were also punished rather harshly. They firmly

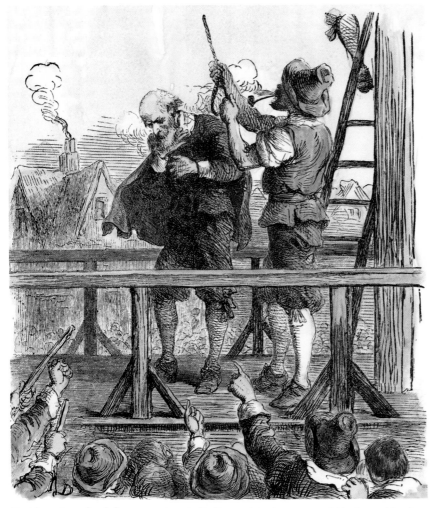

Punishment was harsh for many crimes in Puritan society. A person could be hanged just for practicing another religion (*North Wind Picture Archives*).

believed that God's people had to act in a "godly" manner. Colony members were encouraged to watch each other to make sure no one acted improperly. They thought of this as helping, not hurting their neighbors. They believed, after all, that a person must mean well if he or she wanted to save a neighbor's soul.

What of beliefs of witchcraft? Partly this was handed down from the Middle Ages, when people commonly believed in the existence of demons. These "crude" beliefs seem strange when one considers that the Puritans were also interested in modern science; they wrote about it and even experimented with it.

Witchcraft hysteria gripped Salem, Massachusetts, at the end of the seventeenth century (*North Wind Picture Archives*).

How could they hold such different kinds of beliefs at the same time? It is hard for us to understand.

The last major outburst against "witches" was in the Salem, Massachusetts, area in the late seventeenth century. This incident finally turned people against the idea that fellow colonists could be in league with the devil. By then, the absolute power of the ministers was weakening, and toleration was growing. Also gaining acceptance was the notion that laws should be based on certain human rights and not on what one group of men thought the Bible said.

The excerpt that follows lists a number of laws and codes that governed the Puritans early in their settlement (abbreviations and numbers to the left refer to books, chapters, and verses in the Bible). As we have discussed, these guidelines and punishments grew not out of human rights, but out of a strict and unyielding religious dedication.

94. Capitall Laws

1

Deut. 13. 6, 10   If any man after legal conviction shall have or worship any other god, but the lord god, he shall be put to death.

2

Ex. 22. 18
Lev. 20. 27
Deut. 18. 10   If any man or woeman be a witch, (that is hath or consulteth with a familiar spirit,) They shall be put to death.

3

Lev. 24. 15. 16 If any person shall Blaspheme
the name of god, the father,
Sonne or Holie ghost, with
direct, expresse, presump-
tuous or high handed
blasphemie, or shall curse
god in the like manner, he
shall be put to death.

From: *The Colonial Laws of Massachusetts*, W. H. Whitmore, ed. (Boston: 1889).

Mary Bedwell was one of the many women in Puritan society who was punished for disobeying the strict rules of conduct set out for her by the "elect." In the passage that follows, her "crime" and punishment are described by a witness who attended Bedwell's sentencing in Boston during the mid-1600s.

A Woman Found Guilty

Mary Bedwell bound over to answer for her keeping company and being too familiar with Walter Hickson, of which she was convicted in court. The court sentenced her to sit in the stocks two hours and to be whipped with fifteen stripes or to pay forty shillings in money as a fine to the county and fees of court standing committed until the sentence be performed and if at any time here-after she be taken in company of the said Walter Hickson without other company to be forthwith apprehended by the Constable and to be whipped with ten stripes.

From: *Collections*, Part I, 1671–1680. Publications of the Colonial Society of Massachusetts (Boston: 1933).

CHAPTER 3

DISSENTING VOICES

The Mission of Roger Williams

Today we assume that church and state should be separate in our society. This belief is a key part of our constitutional tradition. It is meant to protect against the government enforcing one "right" point of view on its people, thus denying them freedom. Church and state have not always been completely separate in our history. In the Massachusetts Bay Colony, the Puritan churches were the power behind the government. In effect, church and state were one. But oddly enough, the seed of freedom of religion lay within Puritanism. In theory, Puritanism was a rigid way of life, yet, in actual practice, it set the stage for something much more flexible.

In a positive light, Puritanism's stress on education gave people the tools to think independently and to learn about other ideas. And settling on the edge of a vast wilderness made it possible for groups who opposed Puritan rule to move far enough away to worship as they pleased.

Puritanism had come into existence in England as a revolt against the Church of England. Originally, the Puritans wished to purify the Church of England of what they considered "popish practices"—elements in which Anglicanism (the practices and beliefs of the Church of England) was too much like the Roman Catholic Church. Most of these were questions of worship and church organization, but underlying beliefs embodied in these practices were involved, too. The Puritans thought that the Anglicans put too much stress on the sacraments and ritual. They instead believed that sermons, Bible reading, and the experience of being chosen, or "elected," by God were more important. The Puritans likewise believed that having bishops was unnecessary or even undesirable, but the Anglicans maintained the role of bishops as the successors of the Twelve Apostles. Both sides did agree—as did almost everybody then—that the government should support the church. But when the Puritans saw that the government was not going to support their kind of church, they began to stress the rights of individual congregations of "the elect." But what if some Puritans strongly disagreed with others? Why couldn't there be a revolt *within* Puritanism?

There was, and it came early in the history of Massachusetts Bay. Roger Williams (1603–1683), a minister who came to the colony in 1631, preached and wrote that the government of the colony should have nothing at all to do with the way people worshiped their God. Williams was the first to call for the complete separation of church and state.

Leading figures among the other Puritans would have none of this. They saw Williams as a real threat to their power, so they banished him from Massachusetts Bay. For the minister, however, this turned out to be less a punishment than an opportunity. He and his followers migrated to what became Providence, Rhode Island, and established a community where all the members could practice their religion as they saw fit.

These excerpts from a speech Roger Williams gave in 1644 deal with his fight against church control of government. Beyond that, its tone and blunt attack on the evils of tyranny make it sound a good deal like a major document that would not appear for more than a hundred years: the Declaration of Independence.

Roger Williams negotiated with the Native Americans who inhabited the region that would later become Providence, Rhode Island (*North Wind Picture Archives*).

Against the Church

Magistrates, as magistrates, have no power of setting up the form of church government, electing church officers, punishing with church censures, but to see that the church does her duty herein. And on the other side, the churches as churches, have no power (though as members of the commonweal they may have power) of erecting or altering forms of civil government, electing of civil officers, inflicting civil punishments (no not on persons excommunicate) as by deposing magistrates from their civil authority....

...the sovereign, original, and foundation of civil power lies in the people (whom they must needs mean by the civil power distinct from the government set up). And, if so, that a people may erect and establish what form of government seems to them most meet for their civil condition; it is evident that such governments as are by them erected and established have no more power, nor for no longer time, than the civil power or people consenting and agreeing shall betrust them with. This is clear not only in reason but in the experience of all commonweals, where the people are not deprived of their natural freedom by the power of tyrants.

And, if so, that the magistrates receive their power of governing the church from the people, undeniably it follows that a people, as a people, naturally considered (of what nature or nation soever in Europe, Asia, Africa, or America), have fundamentally and originally, as men, a power to govern the church, to see her do her duty, to correct her, to redress, reform, establish, etc.

From: *The History of New England from 1630 to 1649,* Vol. 2, by John Winthrop; James Savage, ed. (Boston: Little, Brown & Co., 1853).

Bacon's Rebellion

To explain his rebellion against the government in 1676, Nathaniel Bacon (1647–1676) wrote "The Declaration of the People." Like Roger Williams's document, it, too, might have been used as a model for the Declaration of Independence of 1776.

As was the case with the Revolutionary War, which began in 1775, Bacon's Rebellion started with the colonists' complaint that a royal government was not acting in their best interests. It occurred in the colony of Virginia, then under the rule of Governor William Berkeley (1606–1677). Berkley ran a corrupt government, raising taxes and wasting what he collected. Then something worse angered the people of Virginia.

Indians often attacked frontier settlements, killing many colonists, but Berkeley didn't send forces to protect the settlers. The colonists felt that Berkeley had held back because he had interests in the fur trade and needed to stay on good terms with the Indians.

Nathaniel Bacon, a member of the Governor's Council and also Berkeley's cousin, came to the aid of the colonists. He had a farm on the frontier and understood the farmers' complaints. Unwilling to wait for a government response, Bacon put together his own force and attacked the Indians. He also demanded that the governor establish a fair tax system that would end corruption.

Berkeley arrested Bacon for "treason," but then pardoned him. Once free, Bacon again raised a military force and this time captured the capital,

Jamestown. While in control, he pushed through new laws limiting the power of government and making it more democratic. There's no telling where Bacon's efforts might have led if he hadn't died suddenly on October 26, 1676. Leaderless, the revolt died with him. Despite its short life, Bacon's movement did form the basis for the eventual strengthening of the House of Burgesses, the body in which Virginia's voters were represented.

Bacon and his followers felt they had to explain why they opposed the government (as did the writers of the Declaration of Independence nearly 100 years later). In the excerpt that follows notice how the "rebels" are claiming that *they* are the ones who are acting in the name of the king, and it is the governor and his men who are the "traitors." By the time the Declaration was actually written—a century later, during the American Revolution—the rebels would no longer need the king's authority to justify their cause or their actions.

The Declaration of the People

For having upon specious pretences of Publick works raised unjust Taxes upon the Commonalty for the advancement of private Favourts and other sinnister ends but noe visible effects in any measure adequate.

For not having dureing the long time of his Government in any measure advanced this hopefull Colony either by Fortification, Townes or Trade.

For having abused and rendered Contemptible the Majesty of Justice, of advancing to places of judicature scandalous and Ignorant favourits.

For having wronged his Majesties Prerogative and Interest by assuming the monopoley of the Beaver Trade.

By having in that unjust gaine Bartered and sould his Majesties Country and the lives of his Loyal Subjects to the Barbarous Heathen.

For haveing protected favoured and Imboldened the Indians against his Majesties most Loyall subjects never contriveing requireing or appointing any due or proper means of satisfaction for their many Invasions Murthers and Robberies Committed upon us.

For haveing the second tyme attempted the same thereby, caling downe our Forces from the defence of the Frontiers, and most weake Exposed Places, for the prevention of civill Mischief and Ruine amongst ourselves, whilst the barbarous Enemy in all places did Invade murder and spoyle us his Majesties most faithfull subjects.

Of these the aforesaid Articles wee accuse S'r William Berkeley, as guilty of each and every one of the same, and as one, who hath Traiterously attempted, violated and Injured his Majesties Interest here, by the losse of a great Part of his Colony, and many of his Faithfull and Loyall subjects by him betrayed, and in a barbarous and shamefull manner exposed to the Incursions and murthers of the Heathen....

And wee doe further demand, That the said S'r William Berkeley, with all the Persons in this List, be forthwith delivered upp, or surrender themselves, within foure dayes, after the notice hereof, or otherwise wee declare, as followeth, That in whatsoever house, place, or shipp, any of the said Persons shall reside, be hide, or protected, Wee doe declare, that the Owners, masters, or Inhabitants of the said places, to be Confederates, and Traitors to the People, and the Estates of them, as alsoe of all the aforesaid Persons to be Confiscated, This wee the Commons of Virginia doe declare desiring a prime Union among ourselves, that wee may Joyntly, and with one Accord defend ourselves against the Common Enemye. And Let not the Faults of the guilty, be the Reproach of the Innocent, or the Faults or Crimes of ye Oppressors divide and separate us, who have suffered by theire oppressions.

These are therefore in his Majesties name, to Command you forthwith to seize, the Persons above mentioned, as Traytors to ye King and Countrey, and them to bring to Middle Plantation, and there to secure them, till further Order, and in Case of opposition, if you want any other Assistance, you are forthwith to demand it in the Name of the People of all the Counties of Virginia.

[signed]
NATH BACON, Gen'l.

By the Consent of ye People.

From: *The Virgina Magazine of History and Biography,* Vol. I (1893).

CHAPTER 4

AFRICAN AMERICANS, NATIVE AMERICANS, AND WOMEN

Bringing Slaves to the New World

Although slavery was frequently called the South's "peculiar institution" during the 1800s, it was by no means an American invention. In order to truly understand America's history with slavery, one must put slavery into its historical perspective throughout the world.

Slavery has existed in almost every civilization throughout the ages. There were slaves in ancient Rome, as there were in Europe during the Middle Ages. When European slave traders arrived on the shores of Africa in the 1500s, they were often met by African tribal leaders who were eager to barter their slaves for material goods such as gold, guns, and beads. For much of the world, slave trading was a widespread, very profitable, and very popular business. Because it had been in existence for so long—and because it had been a part of everyday life in so many cultures—few

During the 1500s and 1600s, African males were often captured by warriors of rival tribes and then sold to European slave traders (*North Wind Picture Archives*).

people even considered that there might be something morally wrong with the whole idea.

The international slave trade reached grand proportions during the sixteenth century, when large oceangoing slave ships made slavery big business. In the excerpt that follows, a typical sixteenth-century slave-trading journey is described. The story centers around John Hawkins, a well-known trader with a rather colorful reputation throughout the New World.

The ship John Hawkins sailed on was called the *Jesus of Lubeck*. Did anyone think it strange—as we would today—that a ship with such a name be used to transport slaves? The answer is that most people of that day did not think as we do about slavery. Most people did not consider it wrong at all.

For one thing, those who supported the slave trade assumed that these "primitives" would be better off as slaves because they would be Christianized. This meant that even ministers could find a way to justify the practice. Moreover, as black people with strange customs, Africans were seen not only as different but also as almost a bit less than human, compared with white Europeans. This kind of racism, pure and simple, was not yet subject to widespread criticism.

Europeans could also justify what they were doing because they bought African slaves from other blacks on that continent. Slave buyers thought, if these black slave traders had no problem with what they were doing, why should whites?

Perhaps more than anything, it was greed that caused men to justify the enslavement of other human beings. The Spaniards in the New World desperately needed slave labor to exploit the mines and other sources of wealth they had found, and they paid well for this live cargo.

As it happens, the trip described in the following firsthand account by Hawkins was not very profitable. Spanish warships attacked Hawkins along with Sir Francis Drake (1540–1596)—who was on this particular journey. Though the two captains made it back to England, many of their men didn't. In the process, the expedition also lost several ships, along with the slave cargo aboard them.

Captain Hawkins Describes a Journey

Arrived at Cape Verde the eighteenth of November, where we landed 150 men, hoping to obtain some Negroes: where we got but few and those with great hurt and damage to our men, which chiefly proceeded of their envenomed arrows, and although in the beginning they seemed to be but small hurts, yet there hardly escaped any that had blood drawn of them but died in strange sort, with their mouths shut some ten days before they died and after their wounds were whole; where I myself had one of the greatest wounds yet, thanks be to God, escaped.

...there came to us a Negro, sent from a king oppressed by other kings, his neighbours, desiring our aid, with promise that as many Negroes as by these wars might be obtained, as well of his part as of ours, should be at our pleasure....

Now had we obtained between four and five hundred Negroes, wherewith we thought it somewhat reasonable to seek the coast of the West Indies, and there for our Negroes and other our merchandise we hoped to obtain whereof to countervail our charges with some gains, whereunto we proceeded with all diligence, furnished our watering, took fuel, and departed the coast of Guinea the third of February, continuing at the sea with a passage more hard than before hath been accustomed till the twenty-seventh day of March, which day we had sight of an island called Dominica upon the coast of the West Indies, in 14 degrees; from thence we coasted from place to place, making our traffic with the Spaniards as we might, somewhat hardly, because the King had straitly commanded all his governors in those parts by no means to suffer any trade to be made with us.

From: *The Hawkins' Voyages*, Clement R. Markham, ed. (London: The Hakluyt Society, 1878).

Slavery Takes Hold in the South

African Americans were part of the New World from the start. But their part was chosen for them. Throughout the seventeenth century, they were perhaps farther removed from the center of colonial life than other members of society.

Slavery grew slowly in the Carolinas (a single colony until 1729) because white indentured servants performed much of the hard labor. These were people who agreed to work for several years in return for transportation to America, room and board, and perhaps some land when their term of service was up.

Unlike the situation in Virginia, with its tobacco farms, cattle raising was important in the Carolinas. Slaves there in the early seventeenth century needed to have a certain amount of freedom to move with the cattle from place to place. Blacks were also used to help defend the colony from Indians, so most slaves had to be trusted with guns.

But when the cultivation of rice replaced cattle, the role of slaves in the Carolinas changed. Plantations grew bigger and required more labor until, in 1708, blacks began to outnumber whites. The changing economy brought with it a change in social relations. Whites now regulated the life of the slaves so that the maximum amount of work was produced with a minimum amount of trouble for the masters.

By the beginning of the eighteenth century, Southern planters felt they faced a possibly greater threat from their slaves than from the Indians.

Slaves were delivered to the Jamestown settlement in Virginia as early as 1619 (*Library of Congress*).

White farmers in the South soon decided that, if their way of life was to survive, they would have to impose stronger controls on their slaves.

In step with these ideas, courts produced decisions that tightened the slaves' bonds. One such decision, in 1699, even held that killing a slave while punishing him or her was not illegal. Finally, slave control was written into law, producing slave "codes" like the one that follows.

Slavery Protected by Law

WHEREAS, THE PLANTATIONS and estates of this province cannot be well and sufficiently managed and brought into use, without the labor and service of negroes and other slaves; and...as the said negroes and other slaves brought into the people of this Province for that purpose, are of barbarous, wild, savage natures, and such as renders them wholly unqualified to be governed by the laws, customs, and practices of this Province; but that it is absolutely necessary, that such other constitutions, laws and orders, should in this Province be made and enacted, for the good regulating and ordering of them, as may restrain the disorders, rapines and inhumanity, to which they are naturally prone and inclined, and may also tend to the safety and security of the people of this Province and their estates....

BE IT THEREFORE ENACTED...that all negroes, mulattoes, mestizoes or Indians, which at any time heretofore have been sold, or now are held or taken to be, or hereafter shall be bought and sold for slaves, are hereby declared slaves, and they, and their children, are hereby made and declared slaves.

From: *Who Built America?* Vol. 1, Herbert Gutman, et al., eds. (New York: Pantheon Books, 1992). Reprinted by permission.

Chief Powhatan

Most people who have heard of Powhatan (1550–1618) think of him as the father of Pocahontas, the Indian woman who persuaded the chief not to kill Captain John Smith. Although the truth of that story is in doubt, there is no question that Powhatan was an important man to his people and important to the English colonists who wished to live near his tribe.

Early European settlers tried to communicate with Native Americans in order to maintain peace and friendship. Too often, however, violence erupted between the two groups (*North Wind Picture Archives*).

The English were not exactly sure how to deal with this powerful chief. After all, they did not have much experience with similar relationships or with Native American culture. Toward the end of 1608, the councilors of King James I sent a representative to Virginia to offer Powhatan a copper crown. The plan was for the English to recognize him as king of his people, but under the ultimate authority of the king of England. Captain Smith sent a message to Powhatan that he should come to Jamestown to receive "presents" from the English monarch.

"If your king has sent me presents," the chief replied, "I also am a king and this is my land." He said that the presents should be brought to him. Most likely, suspecting a trick, he added: "Neither will I bite at such a bait."

Powhatan got his way. He accepted the "presents" only when they were brought to him. But as would often happen in the long and tragic history of whites and Native Americans, each side misunderstood the other. By accepting the gifts, the English thought the chief had accepted the authority of James I. But Powhatan took the offerings to mean simply that one king sent gifts to another—on an equal basis.

There could be no misunderstanding, however, about the aggressive attempts by the English to establish their colony. Powhatan clearly understood where the relationship between the English and the Native Americans was headed. In the following excerpt, recorded in 1609, Powhatan asks the foreigners to stop and think about the consequences of their aggressive colonization of Indian land. The settlers, however, did not heed him, and in 1622 Powhatan's people massacred many of them.

Many of Jamestown's settlers were killed in the massacre of 1622 (*Library of Congress*).

Powhatan's speech to Captain John Smith is very moving and clear. Did Indians really speak English this beautifully?

We know that public speaking was important to Native Americans. Theirs was an "oral culture": news, stories, and information all came by the spoken word. Saying something well was a valued skill, as the following excerpt shows.

Powhatan Speaks

I have seen two generations of my people die. Not a man of the two generations is alive now but myself. I know the difference between peace and war better than any man in my country. I am now grown old, and must die soon; my authority must descend to my brothers, Opitchapan, Opechan-canough and Catatough;—then to my two sisters, and then to my two daughters. I wish them to know as much as I do, and that your love to them may be like mine to you. Why will you take by force what you may have quietly by love? Why will you destroy us who supply you with food? What can you get by war? We can hide our provisions and run into the woods; then you will starve for wrong-ing your friends. Why are you jealous of us? We are unarmed, and willing to give you what you ask, if you come in a friendly manner, and not with swords and guns, as if to make war upon an enemy. I am not so simple as not to know that it is much better to eat good meat, sleep comfortably, live quietly with my wives and children, laugh and be merry with the English, and trade for their copper and hatchets, than to run away from them, and to lie cold in the woods, feed on acorns, roots and such trash, and be so hunted that I can neither eat nor sleep. In these wars, my men must sit up watching, and if a twig break, they all cry out, "Here comes Captain Smith!" So I must end my miserable life. Take away your guns and swords, the cause of all our jealousy, or you may all die in the same manner.

From: *Lives of Celebrated American Indians* by Samuel Goodrich (Boston: Bradbury, Soden,1843).

William Penn

William Penn
(*National Portrait
Gallery*).

William Penn's (1644–1718)
approach to dealing with the Indians might be called
"the road not taken." Although he was not the only
white settler in this period to treat the Indians fairly
and equally, Penn was not typical of his time.

Penn knew from experience just how important
it was to tolerate those who seemed different. In
England, where he was born into a well-off family, he
had become a member of the Society of Friends—the
Quakers. Of all the major organized branches of Prot-
estantism that took hold in England, this was the most
democratic. The Quakers stressed the importance of
each person's own conscience, even when conscience

and the law came into conflict. They were strictly pacifists, and would not fight even if they were ordered to do so by the government.

As a Quaker, William Penn went to prison for his beliefs. He decided that people like him needed a refuge where they could freely practice their religion without fear of persecution. Unlike the Puritans, he also pictured this place as one where those who had fled from persecution, once in the majority, would not try to impose their views on others.

This place of refuge was founded on the settlement of a debt. King Charles owed Penn's father money. In 1681, the crown paid the debt by granting William Penn the land that would become part of the state of Pennsylvania (the name means "Penn's woods"). The new owner sailed to his colony in 1682, settled there, and wrote laws for it that would later become a model of American democracy.

Penn's 1682 treaty of friendship with the Indians worked until well into the next century. It was then that the Quakers in Pennsylvania lost control of the colony to other settlers—a growing number of whites put pressure on the supply of available land. Here, as elsewhere in America, Native Americans would be pushed aside to make room for colonial settlement.

For Penn, the "love" frequently mentioned in this document was an active principle by which he lived. He did not use the term loosely or talk about it because it sounded good. Upon reading his words, one might wonder how different our history might have been if more whites had approached the Native Americans with an active and peaceful friendship, as William Penn did.

William Penn's Handwritten Treaty with the Indians

The Great God who is the power and wisdom that made you and inclines your hearts to righteousness, love, and peace. This I send to inform you of my love and to desire your love to my friends, and [those] whom the Great God brings among you. I intend to order all things in good manner that we may all live in love and peace one with another which I hope the Great God will incline both me and you to do. I seek nothing but the honor of His praise, and that we who are his workmanship, may do that which I hope is well pleasing to him. The man which delivers this unto you, is my special friend. Sober, kind, and loving, you may believe him. I have already taken care that none of my people wrong you, by good laws. I have provided for that purpose, and will, never allow any of my people to sell Rum to make your people drunk. If anything should be out of order, report when I come, it shall commandeer, and I will bring you some things of our Country that are wonderful and pleasing to you. So I rest in Love of our god who made us. I am

Your Loving Friend
Wm. Penn
England 25 : 2 : 1682

From: Original handwritten source, Library of Congress. (Transcribed by Blackbirch Graphics: Woodbridge, CT, 1993.)

Benjamin Colman on
His Daughter, Jane

T he records of the New England colonies tell us very little about what life was like for women in the seventeenth and early eighteenth centuries. Unless they broke the law and their punishment was recorded, we usually know only when they were born, when they married, and when they died.

Women did not preach sermons that were later printed, nor were they likely to sign business agreements. They did not fill leadership posts in colonial governments, nor did they attend Harvard College. Few books or published works had female authors. Women were expected to manage the home, read their Bible, and remain submissive to their husbands. They were also helpmates for their husbands, who carried on life's more "serious" business.

When women did get a chance to write something, it was most likely just to take notes on a preacher's sermon, writing down what a man had said. Because eighteenth century women were so often made to be spectators rather than active participants, we must rely mostly on what men wrote about them. Some of these writings—often printed funeral sermons— suggest that, given a chance, women could have added a great deal to the public life of the colonies.

Benjamin Colman, a minister, left behind a letter to his daughter, Jane, which is excerpted here. The minister hints at how society suffered by not allowing women to participate in many aspects of life.

Jane Colman grew up at the beginning of the eighteenth century. She read books in her father's library and wrote poetry. When Massachusetts Bay's greatest minister, Cotton Mather (1663–1728), died, she praised his life in writing.

Colonial women in New England had strictly defined roles. They were expected to maintain their homes, feed their families, and follow the moral codes prescribed in the Bible (*North Wind Picture Archives*).

As is clear from his letter, Benjamin Colman appreciated his daughter's talents. Just as clear is his belief that it would not have been proper for her to put her mind to use the way he had his own. Considering this, he simply advises her to keep practicing her skills and to improve herself. Unfortunately, there was a physical limit to how far his daughter could pursue her independence. Like many women of her time, Jane Colman died during childbirth in 1735, deprived of a full life as well as full opportunity.

A "Woman's Place"

My poor Gift is in thinking and writing with a little Eloquence, and a Poetical turn of Thought. This, in proportion to the Advantages you have had, under the necessary and useful Restraints of your Sex, you enjoy to the full of what I have done before you. With the Advantages of my liberal Education at School & Colege, I have no reason to think but that your Genious in Writing would have excell'd mine. But there is no great Progress or Improvement ever made in any thing but by Use and Industry and Time. If you diligently improve your stated and some vacant hours every Day or Week to read your bible and other useful Books, you will...grow in knowledge and Wisdom, fine tho'ts and good Judgment.

From: *Reliquiae Turellae, et Lachrymae Paternae* by Benjamin Colman (Boston: S. Kneeland and T. Green, 1735).

King Philip's War

By the late seventeenth century, it had become clear that the growth of the New England colonies would not allow for separate white and Native American dominions. One or the other would win out, dominate the entire area, and move the other aside. In the end, it came down to a matter of who had more men and weapons.

Whites had often paid the Indians for land, but Native Americans did not usually have the choice of whether or not to sell. Sometimes whites simply seized the land they wanted or made alliances, playing one tribe off against the other. Whites gained land by going to war as allies of one tribe against an enemy tribe.

In 1675, tensions between whites and Indians reached a climax. Native Americans, feeling that their very survival was at stake, struck back at whites in full force, and the result was King Philip's War.

King Philip (1639–1676) became the chief of the Wampanoags in 1662, succeeding his brother who had recently succeeded his father, Massosoit. Determined to show the Indians who was in control, the settlers of the Plymouth Colony treated the new chief with little respect. In 1675, someone murdered an Indian who had told the whites that Philip was planning to attack. The whites accused Philip of the crime, but he denied it. In a series of small incidents that grew steadily worse, whites attacked Indians, who then rose up against settlers in retaliation. Other tribes and other colonies got drawn in, and soon it was a major war.

King Philip, Chief of the Wampanoags (*Library of Congress*).

The following selection from a book published in London in 1676 tells the settlers' side of the story. It describes Indians who behave "savagely," stopping at nothing to destroy and terrorize whites. It is important to remember that whites often treated the Indians with an equal lack of mercy. The Indians felt this brutality was justified because they were convinced that the settlers would do the same to them if they were not stopped.

The settlers had the advantage of having Native American allies, even in this war. The conflict ended when one of these Indians killed King Philip in August 1676. Casualties during the war have been estimated at 3,000 Indians and 600 whites. In addition, Indian tribal power was put down, never to rise again in this part of North America.

Editor's Note: *When reading this excerpt, keep in mind that in most cases the letter* f *should be read as* s.

A White View of Indians

The *Indians* began to appear abroad again as mifchievous as ever; For the very next week they fet upon *Lancafter Town*, killed feveral people, and carried away many prifoners; Such houfes as were fortified, defended themfelves, but the greateft part of the Town they fired and plundered; and had deftroyed the whole place, had not Captain *Wadfworth* upon hearing of the Guns come with great expedition from *Sudbury*, with a party to their relief; After this they cut off a farm-houfe near *Sudbury*, killed feven people in a barbarous manner, and carried fome away captive: Three hundred of them fet upon the Town of *Maidesfield*, and burnt at leaft fifty Houfes, killed and took divers of the Inhabitants, being all furprifed before they were aware....

Their next Attempt (I mean of any confiderable Body of the *Indians*) was upon a Town called *Nafhaway*, which they fet fire to, and burnt down to the ground; There was little refiftance made here, people endeavouring rather to efcape their Fury by flight then oppofition; and yet they killed many, burnt the Town down to the ground, and took no leffe then five and fifty perfons into their mercileffe Captivity.... As they were leading them away in this lamentable condition, one of the Sifters being big with childe, going into the Woods to be privately delivered, the *Indians* followed, and in a jeering manner, they would help her, and be her Midwives, and thereupon they barbaroufly ript up her body, and burnt the childe before her face, and then in a mercifull cruelty, to put her out of her pain, knockt her o'th head.

From: *A Thankful Remembrance of God's Mercy* (Cambridge, England: 1676).

Although some of the first Europeans who came to America did not survive the harsh challenges of settlement, many did. Those who were able to endure the ravages of cold winters, the constant outbreak of infectious diseases, and the frequent conflicts with the Native Americans managed to create prosperous and relatively harmonious societies. By the 1760s, these colonists would assert their independence and fight England for the right to govern themselves without interference. Their victory in the Revolution was the final step in declaring these colonies their own.

EUROPE MEETS THE NEW WORLD: 1492–1682

1492
Italian navigator Christopher Columbus discovers the Americas after making his historic voyage across the Atlantic Ocean from Europe.

1513
Explorer Juan Ponce de León discovers Florida, which he names after the Spanish words for Easter, *Pascua Florida.*

1607
The first permanent settlement in North America, Jamestown, is established along the Atlantic coastline.

1614
Pocahontas, a compassionate Native American who tried to encourage peace with European settlers, marries Englishman John Rolfe.

1619
Twenty Africans are brought to Jamestown to be sold to white settlers: slavery begins in North America.

1622
Native Americans, angry about how they are being treated by settlers, attack areas around Jamestown. Many colonists are killed.

1630
Approximately 850 Puritans set sail from England to find religious freedom in the New World.

1675
A series of bloody battles between Native Americans and settlers breaks out, beginning what has been called King Philip's War.

1682
Quaker William Penn creates a treaty of friendship with Native Americans in Pennsylvania. The treaty maintains peace well into the next century.

FOR FURTHER READING

Anderson, Joan. *Christopher Columbus: From Vision to Voyage.* New York: Dial Books for Young Readers, 1991.

Blassingame, Wyatt. *Ponce de León.* New York: Chelsea House, 1991.

Fradin, Dennis B. *King Philip: Indian Leader.* Hillside, NJ: Enslow Publishers, 1990.

Fritz, Jean. *The Double Life of Pocahontas.* North Bellmore, NY: Marshall Cavendish, 1991.

Holler, Anne. *Chief Powhatan and Pocahontas.* New York: Chelsea House, 1993.

Leon, George. *Explorers of the Americas Before Columbus.* New York: Franklin Watts, 1990.

Meltzer, Milton. *Columbus and the World Around Him.* New York: Franklin Watts, 1990.

Roman, Joseph. *King Philip.* New York: Chelsea House, 1992.

Siegel, Beatrice. *A New Look at the Pilgrims: Why They Came to America.* New York: Walker and Company, 1987.

Tames, Richard. *Planters, Pilgrims and Puritans.* Pomfret, VT: Trafalgar Square, 1987.

INDEX

64